Observation:
The Key to Responsive Teaching

Workbook with DVD

Charlotte Stetson
Judy Jablon
Amy Laura Dombro

Teaching Strategies, Inc.
Washington, DC

The publisher and the authors cannot be held responsible for injury, mishap, or damages incurred during the use of or because of the information in this book. The authors recommend appropriate and reasonable supervision at all times based on the age and capability of each child.

Editor: Toni Bickart
Cover Design: Abner Nieves
Layout/Production: Jeff Cross

Teaching Strategies, Inc.
P.O. Box 42243
Washington, DC 20015
www.TeachingStrategies.com
ISBN: 978-1-933021-91-1

Library of Congress Control Number: 2008938668

Printed and bound in the United States of America
2014 2013 2012 2011 2010 2009 2008

10 9 8 7 6 5 4 3 2 1

Table of Contents

Acknowledgments

Observation: The Key to Responsive Teaching began as a dream of Charlotte's. After reading *The Power of Observation* written by Judy and Amy with Margo Dichtelmiller, Charlotte felt that what teachers needed next was an opportunity to practice observing to hone their skills.

That meant a DVD and a chance to work again with Murray Hill Studios. We thank our producer, Shaun Johnsen, for his patience, meticulous attention to detail, artistry, and insight into the content that stems from being the father of Darrien, a lucky little boy. We are also deeply appreciative of Jahaneen Johnsen, Marc Wein, Paul Chappell, and Molly O'Donnell for their kindness, support, facilitation, and attentiveness. We also thank Jim Turner, Bernard Moor-Jamkowski, Neculai Burghelea, and Juan Costello, our outstanding film crew.

It would have been impossible to create this DVD without the cooperation of the many individuals in programs that share our belief that observing is the key to responsive teaching. We thank the staff, families, and children of The Rockefeller Child and Family Center. Dr. Marjorie Goldsmith, the director, and Assistant Directors, Jenn McGregor and Teresa Outlaw-Johnson made extraordinary efforts to help us meet our deadline. We are grateful to the infant and toddler teachers who shared their day with us and the film crew: Colleen Krowl, Luann Ottley, and Francia Garcia in the Violet room; Emily Diaz and Taisha Reyes in the Pink room; Alexa Pomales, Elaine Perez-Rojas, and Tara Wisienski in the Orange room; and Eric Van Felix. We also want to express our gratitude to two parents who appear in the DVD: Heather King and Jyoti Jaiswal.

We extend deep appreciation to the children and teachers in the programs for 4- to 5-year-olds who welcomed us into their classrooms: Sharon Gambrell and Sue Mata from Grace Child Care Center in Perth Amboy, NJ; Lynn Geiger and Ramonita Falcon from the Ignacio Cruz Early Childhood Center in Perth Amboy, NJ; Adam Goldberg, Paula Bosques, and Wilmarie Nieves also from the Ignacio Cruz Early Childhood Center in Perth Amboy, NJ; Louis Mark Romei, Marta Dlugosz, Jodie Charney, and Hope Koslowski from the James A. Garfield Early Childhood Learning Center in Garfield, NJ; Nory Rodriquez, Jessica Casanova, Ruth Enriquez, and Tina Barnet from the ABC Echo Park Early Childhood Head Start Center in New York, NY; Carol Aghayan, Jamie Ourso, Kamille Joubert, and Kate Darbonne, from the Louisiana State University School of Human Ecology Child Development Laboratory Preschool in Baton Rouge, LA. We also extend our appreciation to the administrators: MaryJo Sperlazza, Joan Maldoney, Cindy Shields, Frank D'Amico, Sally Bulger, and Beatrix Mendez; Mary Ellen Rooney, Clarissa Laurente, Dr. Diane Burts, and Dr. Joan Benedict.

We are grateful for the support we received from Teaching Strategies Inc. Toni Bickart, Vice President, Jeff Cross, graphic designer, and Abner Nieves, cover designer, provided valuable editing, advice, and a design that made our words easily accessible to busy teachers.

Finally, we acknowledge, with appreciation and respect, all the children, families, and teachers who have taught us so much over the years.

Charlotte Stetson, Judy Jablon, Amy Laura Dombro

October, 2008

The Why and How of Observing

Do these comments sound familiar?

I know I should be observing more, but it feels unnatural. I can't seem to figure out how to make it a part of my teaching.

It is so hard to free myself from my agenda and take the time needed to really get to know children.

I am a good observer. I watch all the time, see lots of interesting things, and try to take notes. But what do I do with them? How do I apply what I learn to my daily interactions and planning.

These words express the feelings of many teachers and providers we have met over the years. They also reflect our own experiences as teachers. Even after 30 years each in the field, we continue to learn about observing. We wrote this Workbook, *Observation: The Key to Responsive Teaching* because we believe that all of us can become better observers and use the information we learn from observing more effectively. We invite you to join us in exploring the why and how of observing with this Workbook and DVD.

We define observation as watching and listening to learn about individual children. When you make watching and listening to children a purposeful and intentional part of your teaching, you better understand what children are feeling, thinking, and learning. When this understanding guides the decisions you make throughout the day, you become a more responsive teacher. Your work with children and families is more successful and rewarding.

Why Observe?

Responding to the strengths and needs of each child requires you to observe carefully and with intention. We answer the question, "Why Observe?" by explaining four reasons:

- I'm curious about children and want to understand them better.

- I want to get to know each child and build positive relationships.

- I want to find out about each child's development and learning.

- I want to teach more responsively.

Let's take a brief look at each of these reasons to observe and how they are related. You will have a chance to explore each reason in more detail as you engage in the exercises in this Workbook.

Curiosity

Observing with purpose and intention requires you to slow your pace and let yourself be curious about children. Whether you are new to teaching or a veteran, maintaining an attitude of wonder about children means asking questions such as, "What is this child like? and "How does this child respond in different situations?"

Relationships

The information you gain from observing helps you connect with children and build relationships with them and their families. Respectful, sensitive, nurturing relationships with each child and family are a prerequisite to helping a child grow and learn. Strong relationships develop from knowing children extremely well. When you observe, you gather details about each child that leads to respect and appreciation, the hallmarks of positive relationships.

Development and Learning

As you form strong positive relationships with children, your curiosity about them is likely to increase. Asking questions about children's development and learning leads to a deeper understanding of them. Finding out how each child grows and learns is the third powerful motivation to observe.

Observing for these three reasons leads to the fourth and most complex reason: responsive teaching.

Responsive Teaching

Observing gives you information you need to make decisions so you can respond to children thoughtfully rather than simply react. This greatly increases the chances that what you say and do to guide children's development and learning will bring positive results.

With these four reasons in mind, let's look at **how** to observe.

How to Observe

We think about the practice of observing with intention as an ongoing cycle with four phases.

1. **Ask questions.** The cycle begins when you ask questions and wonder about children.

2. **Watch, listen, and record.** In this next phase, you watch closely and listen carefully to gather information to help answer your questions. You record factual notes to remember what you see children do and say.

3. **Reflect.** In the third phase, you pause to think about the significance of what you see and hear, and your reactions to it. In this book we refer to this phase as having a mini-conversation with yourself.

4. **Respond.** Having paused to reflect, you now decide how to respond. Based on your reflections, you might decide to respond immediately, or at a later time.

Then the cycle repeats. Regardless of why you observe, you always proceed through the four phases. Sometimes you move through these four phases quickly. You might go through the cycle several times during a single interaction with a child. At other times, you move through the phases more slowly and over a longer period of time.

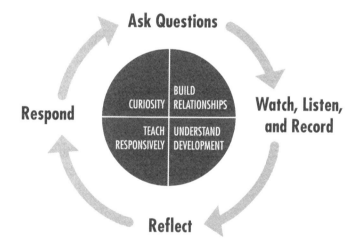

Looking Ahead

You may work directly with children as a family child-care provider, a caregiver, or a Head Start, preschool, or kindergarten teacher. Perhaps you are a staff developer or work in a college setting. Because we believe that children grow and learn when they are with you, we use *teacher* throughout the book to refer to you.

We hope that this Workbook and DVD offer you these opportunities:

*   Validate and build on what you already know about observing.

*   Practice observing children and teachers in natural settings.

*   Sharpen existing skills and develop new ones in a series of guided exercises.

*   Share your questions and discoveries with colleagues.

The Workbook

Chapter 1 sets the stage by describing the four reasons to observe, the four phases of the observation cycle, and how to use the book.

Chapters 2–5 each begin with an explanation of one reason to observe followed by a vignette illustrating a teacher in action observing for this reason. Then there are four exercises, each one focusing on one phase of the observation cycle:

- Ask questions
- Watch, listen, record
- Reflect
- Respond

The exercises are accompanied by DVD clips. Each exercise is structured in three parts: before watching, while watching, and after watching.

In chapter 6 you have an opportunity to engage in a self-assessment process and determine your next steps in the ongoing process of becoming an effective observer and a responsive teacher.

Two appendices follow:

- Appendix A is a list of all the exercises in the book and the DVD clips that accompany them.
- Appendix B includes resources and references. The resources are organized by topic. The first section is a general selection of books about observation. The next four sections are grouped according to the reasons to observe.

The DVD

The DVD that accompanies this book has thirteen clips, each clip 2–6 minutes in length. A menu appears at the beginning of the DVD that identifies the clips by number (1–13) and name. You can click on the name and go directly to the clip that accompanies the exercise. A frame at the beginning of each clip tells its number and name. Many clips have multiple segments identified also by number and name, e.g., Segment 12.4, "Max and Emily, Age 4." Sometimes you will be prompted to pause the tape between segments.

Each clip on the DVD is linked to a specific exercise in the book. As you engage in the exercises, we encourage you to watch the clips more than once. Often, you will see things during a second or third viewing that you missed the first time around. Even though you cannot replay a particular event in real life, viewing a clip several times is an excellent way to sharpen your eyes, attune your ears, and become a more skilled observer!

Options for Using the Workbook and DVD

Observation: The Key to Responsive Teaching may be used in conjunction with another Teaching Strategies' publication, *The Power of Observation. The Power of Observation* offers ideas and inspiration for getting started as an observer of young children. It provides a strong background for the work you will be doing as you watch each video clip and complete the exercises in this book. *Observation: The Key to Responsive Teaching* provides a series of exercises to give teachers practice and guidance as they grow as observers. The final pages of chapters 2–6 include guidance on where to find additional information about the topic in *The Power of Observation*.

On you own. You may want to practice and improve your observation skills. As you engage in the exercises, we encourage you to take ample time to reflect, think, and record your thoughts and feelings. Whenever possible, check in with a friend or colleague to share your experiences.

With colleagues. Maybe you and two or three colleagues have formed a learning team to work on developing your observation skills. You can discuss ideas and strategies with each other, support each other as questions and issues arise, and acknowledge each other's progress.

In a multi-week college course. You will find that the 16 exercises and the suggestions for reflection and discussion can guide learning over the course of a semester. *The Power of Observation* may serve as additional required reading.

For staff meetings and workshops. The sequence and structure of *Observation: The Key to Responsive Teaching* lends itself to planning professional development opportunities.

We encourage you to try the exercises over several weeks to give you time to practice. Allow at least one week in between exercises, or perhaps even more. Please DO NOT do all sixteen exercises at once! Not only would your attention fade after two or three of them, you would lose the benefit of time in between the exercises to practice and apply each lesson in your work.

We are pleased that you have chosen to use *Observation: The Key to Responsive Teaching* to guide your continuing journey to be a skillful observer and we hope that you find it useful. As you try the strategies offered in the book, make observing your own powerful resource. Create forms that work for you. Find colleagues with whom to share ideas. Be energized by the daily successes you have and avoid being discouraged when the work is difficult. Take a deep breath and use observation as a way to reap the full rewards of your work with children and families.

I'm Curious

Good teachers are curious, life-long learners. They know there is always something new to learn about children, families, and teaching. Curiosity about children, the desire to understand how they experience their world, motivates us to observe and keeps our work interesting.

The vignette and exercises in this chapter focus on curiosity as the reason to observe.

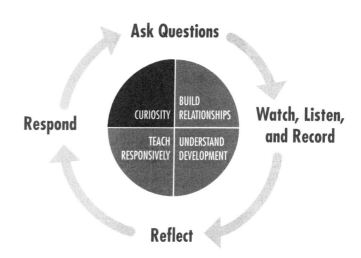

Monique's Story

Here is a story about Monique, an infant/toddler teacher. As you read her story, notice how curiosity motivates her to observe and learn something new about Jarwin. Perhaps you will see yourself reflected in her story.

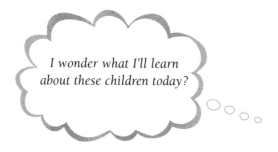

I wonder what I'll learn about these children today?

As Monique opens the door to the infant-toddler room, it is quiet and still. She takes a deep breath and sips from her mug of coffee. Morning is her favorite time in the room; she likes seeing it gradually come to life as the first few children arrive to begin a new day. As she moves across the room to begin her preparations, she glances at the display of contact-paper-covered photographs of the children on the wall. She pauses briefly to look at each child's face for a few seconds.

Soon, 6-month-old Jarwin arrives with his dad. Jarwin's expressive eyes have always fascinated Monique. She has learned that she can read his emotions just by looking at his eyes. Today however, she finds herself paying attention to Jarwin's hands as he clutches a rattle in one and a piece of banana in the other.

This is an exciting development! I've never seen him hold something in each hand at the same time!

After sitting Jarwin in the beanbag chair, Jarwin's father begins stashing his bottles in the refrigerator. Monique kneels in front of Jarwin and shares her observation with him. "Look at that—you have a rattle in one hand and some banana in the other...my first note of the day for your observation chart!"

I really want to remember this.

Jarwin smiles and watches Monique write a quick note on her clipboard before she asks Jarwin's dad, "Have you and Francine seen him hold two things in his hands before? It seems to me he usually needs both hands to hold onto one thing. His fingers and hands must be getting a little bigger and stronger!"

This was such a surprise! I need to pay attention to what he can do with his hands.

Jarwin's dad leaves for work. Monique sticks the note on Jarwin's observation chart, picks him up, walks into the storage closet, and collects some interesting objects, all the right size to fit into Jarwin's hands. She puts them in a basket that she places on the floor as she sits beside him. She adds a note to his plan for the week: *Offer Jarwin things to hold in each hand at the same time.*

I'll be interested to see what he does with all the different things we give him to hold!

What is your reaction to Monique's story?

What do you find interesting?

Do you see yourself in the story? If so, how?

Do you have a story to tell about observing because you were curious?

Practice Observing: I'm Curious

The observation cycle begins with asking questions. As you watch children, what do you wonder about? Maybe you wonder about what they love to do or their personalities. Perhaps you wonder what **they** are curious about!

> *You learn something every day if you pay attention.*
>
> Rosa, teacher of 3-year-olds

Ask Questions Because I'm Curious

 For this exercise, watch all the segments of Clip 1, "A Collage of Young Children."

Before watching

Consider these questions:

What fascinates you about young children?

Do you find yourself watching them at the grocery store, the laundromat, or as they play in the park? Recall a recent situation where you stopped what you were doing to pay attention to a child because you were curious to see what he or she was going to do next.

While watching

Notice what attracts you, makes you smile or laugh. Think about what interests or puzzles you about this series of short film segments showing children from the age of 4 months to 5 years.

After watching

Record your responses to these questions:

What made you smile or laugh?

What did you wonder about?

What kept you interested?

What questions do you have about these children?

For the next few weeks, as you go about your day, notice what attracts your attention as you watch young children. What is it about them that causes you to smile, laugh, wonder, or stare? What do you find interesting? Record your thoughts here.

Watch, Listen, and Record to Keep Track of What I Notice

As you watch and listen to children, it helps to record what you see and hear so that you can remember what you find particularly intriguing or significant. Writing brief, factual notes provides you with a record of the interesting things children say and do.

Each of us brings our interests, preferences, and ways of seeing to the act of observing. In this exercise we encourage you to notice what you pay attention to when you observe.

 Watch Clip 2, "Eliana, Age 4," Segment 2.1, "Eliana Draws During Choice Time."

Before watching

Consider the idea that what attracts our attention first is what we are most likely to remember. Think about yourself and these questions:

What do you notice most when you observe children?

How do they move?

What expressions are on their faces?

How do they use language?

While watching

Focus on 4-year-old Eliana's hands, eyes, and facial expressions. The chart that follows will help you keep track of what you see. Record a few words about how she uses each of these parts of her body. Write only what you see and avoid unnecessary words. An example is included to give you an idea of what you might write. Try to add a few notes related to each question.

What does she do with her hands?	*Uses L hand to turn paper, holds cap in L hand while holding top of page. Draws w/ R hand.*
Where does she focus her eyes?	
What expressions show on her face?	

After watching

Talk with others if you can and share the words you recorded. Respond to these questions:

How many words did you write?

Could you eliminate some and still remember what you saw?

What was it like to pay close attention to different aspects of a child's actions? What was easy? Hard?

If you are working with others, what are the similarities and differences among what people noticed?

What insights do you take from this exercise?

For the next few weeks, try to pay closer attention to how children move different parts of their bodies, what they look at, and their facial expressions. Try writing a few brief notes.

Reflect to Make Sense of What I See

The third phase of the observation cycle is reflection, the mini-conversation you have with yourself. It might take three seconds or five minutes but the important thing is that you pause and think about the significance of what you have observed.

Before continuing on to the exercises, look back at Monique's story. As you read it again, notice how her thoughts reveal the conversations she has with herself.

 Watch Clip 2, "Eliana, Age 4," Segment 2.1, "Eliana Draws During Choice Time," again. The focus this time is your thinking. Slow down and try to keep track of your thoughts as you watch.

Before watching

Take a minute to consider these questions:

Are you aware of having an internal conversation with yourself as you observe?

Is this a new idea for you? What are your reactions to the concept of reflection as a mini-conversation with yourself?

While watching

Keep track of your thoughts as you watch Eliana for a second time. Write them here.

After watching

Think about these questions. If you are working with others, share and compare your responses to these questions:

Were you aware of a conversation with yourself as you watched Eliana? If so, what were you thinking?

As you reflect on what you saw, do you have new questions about Eliana?

During the next few days take time to reflect as you observe children. Pay attention to your thoughts about their actions and words.

Respond to Further My Curiosity

Your reflections guide how you respond. We often think of a response as an action the teacher takes directly with a child. Our instinct as teachers is to step in and do something, especially when we see a child working alone, grappling with a problem, or doing something that we do not understand.

When you do not quite understand what is happening or what exactly is the best strategy to try, give yourself permission to remain curious so that you can learn more. In this case your responses may be invisible to the child but powerful in terms of their impact. Here are some options:

- Continue observing and documenting as you watch and listen to keep learning about the child.

- Make a plan to observe in a different situation to see the child's behavior in another context.

- Ask a family member a question to get more information related to what you saw and heard.

 Watch Clip 2, "Eliana, Age 4," Segment 2.2, "Eliana With Puppets."

Before watching
Think about your own observation experiences. Consider these questions:

Think of a situation in which you decided to continue observing and documenting to keep learning about the child. Why did you make this decision?

Think of a situation in which you decided to make a plan to observe in another setting. Why did you make this decision?

Think of a situation in which you decided to ask a family member a question to get more information. Why did you make this decision?

While watching

Keep in mind three ways you could decide to respond in order to learn more about Eliana:

Keep watching Eliana in this situation.

Make a plan to observe in another situation.

Ask a family member a question.

After watching

Think about what you saw. Consider the direction you would take and why. Discuss your responses with a colleague. Consider situations and reasons in which you might choose to respond in each way. Record them here.

Make a point of trying each of the three responses that you practiced in this exercise. What did you actually do? What happened and what did you learn?

I decided to keep on observing and documenting.

I made a plan to observe in another situation.

I chose to ask a family member a question.

What Did I Learn?

What do you want to remember from this chapter about the influence of curiosity on observing and teaching?

By focusing on children, by really attending to what they do, what they're working on, we bring their world into greater focus (Leipzig, 1988).

Where Can I Learn More?

Here are some suggestions from *The Power of Observation* (2nd ed.):

"Beyond a Set of Skills: Observing as an Attitude of Openness," pages 6–8.

"Describe Rather Than Label Children's Behavior," pages 46–47.

"How Do I Organize The Information I Collect?"

"Step One: Write things down in a way that works for you," pages 84–86.

"Step Two: Organize and store your written observations so you can go back and learn from them," pages 86–91.

"Tips for Getting Started: Observing Every Day," pages 143–147.

I Want to Get to Know Children Better

With young children, the most profound learning is likely to happen when there is a strong, positive relationship between you, the child, and the child's family. Positive relationships begin with observing to get to know children well.

Initially, you wonder about every facet of the child. As you watch and listen carefully, regularly, and systematically over time, you gradually gain a deep appreciation and respect for the child as a unique human being.

Ask Questions

Watch, Listen, and Record

Reflect

Respond

CURIOSITY | BUILD RELATIONSHIPS

TEACH RESPONSIVELY | UNDERSTAND DEVELOPMENT

Knowing individual children well enables you to respond to them in nurturing, positive, and dependable ways as you promote their play and learning, guide their behavior, and simply enjoy being together.

Your knowledge of and relationships with children deepen when you build trusting relationships with their families. Observing children together and sharing observation information with each other is an effective way to learn more about each child and strengthen your relationships with families. By working together, you provide children with continuity between home and child care or school in a way that builds their competence and understanding of themselves and their world.

Your efforts to discover the individuality of each and every child by observing will be rewarded. You will be a more effective teacher. Your connections with families will be stronger. And you will find more satisfaction and enjoyment in your work.

> *For me, the slow and steady process of getting to know a child well is deeply satisfying. When we smile together I know I am being more effective as the child's teacher.*
>
> Laura, Kindergarten Teacher

Randy's Story

Randy's story highlights the connection between observing and building relationships with children and families and how that helps him be a more effective teacher of young children.

Randy is beginning his second year of teaching 3-year-olds in an urban Head Start program. The first year was difficult for him. He worked hard to implement every instructional strategy he learned in college courses and was so busy he felt like he never really got to know all the children in his room. As a result, he felt inadequate as a teacher. Near the end of his first year, he attended a presentation in which he heard Lilian Katz. She said:

> *It's not enough to be amazed by what children do; one must be interested. Amazement is a fleeting kind of "turn on." But interest, by definition, means losing yourself in something outside of yourself, becoming absorbed enough to stay with it over an extended time, to follow up on it, to try to understand it more deeply* (Katz, 2008).

Eager to remember this idea, Randy wrote on a large piece of construction paper "*It's not enough to be amazed by what children do; one must be interested.*" and posted it on the wall of his classroom. As his second year of teaching began, Randy made it a weekly priority to find at least one interesting thing about each child. Soon this decision was making a difference.

During choice time on an October morning, Aida, whose home language is Spanish, hung her nametag on one of the hooks in the dramatic play area as she did at the beginning of nearly every day at choice time. As Randy walked to the block area to observe other children, his eyes landed on Lilian's words. He paused and looked over at Aida, whose limited English made it challenging for him to get to know her. He decided to go to the dramatic play area to observe her playing by herself.

As he approached, he noticed Aida's face. She was in the middle of a long phone conversation alternating between Spanish and English. It seemed that every part of her face was moving. Randy smiled to himself. Her eyebrows were bouncing up and down. Her eyes were alternately closing, squinting, and popping wide open. She squinched her nose, shook her head, smiled, frowned, and grimaced.

Wow, I can't believe I've never noticed Aida's facial expressions before! Her play always looked boring to me. I must not have been paying attention. Maybe it is because I didn't understand her. I had no idea that she knows so many English words.

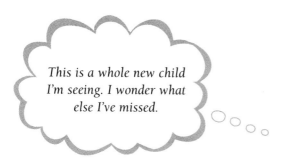

This is a whole new child I'm seeing. I wonder what else I've missed.

He continued watching and jotting notes, focusing on her facial expressions, physical gestures, and use of language. Moving closer to hear her better, but not wanting to interrupt her play, he filled several sticky notes with words describing how she paced around, hunched up her shoulders, gestured with her free hand, changed the tone and volume of her voice, and tried to multi-task as she talked on the phone.

I'll have to share this with her mother this afternoon. She's always telling me that Aida never pays attention to her.

Aida ended her phone conversation by saying, "Okay, I talk to you tomorrow!" Before she got involved in something else, Randy decided to respond by telling Aida what he saw. "Aida," he said, " I heard you on the phone. I could tell by your face that your conversation was really interesting. Do you talk on the telephone at home?"

With a broader grin than he had ever seen before, Aida responded, "No, Mommy talks on her phone!" Randy replied, "Well, Aida, may I call you now?" Together they continued to play.

It's amazing what learning something new about a child can lead to!

The next day, Randy invited another child to join him and Aida to play pretend phone calls. Aida grabbed his hand as they walked together to the dramatic play area.

What is your reaction to Randy's story?

What do you find interesting?

Do you see yourself in the story? If so, how?

Do you have a story to tell about how observing helped you build a trusting relationship with a child?

Practice Observing: I Want to Get to Know Children Better

Initially, you may get to know a child by asking yourself general questions prompted by curiosity. As you continue to observe, the details you learn help you put together a more complete picture of each child. As you see gaps in what you know, your questions and observations become more focused and specific. All of this leads to a better relationship with the child.

> *Observing helps you build relationships by revealing the uniqueness of every child.*
>
> (Jablon, Dombro, & Dichtelmiller, 2007)

Ask Questions to Build Relationships

 We invite you to view Clip 3, "Jenna, Age 3, in a Variety of Situations." Watch Jenna as she arrives at school; works on a puzzle; pumps a ball; washes a rubber animal and sings a song; and washes and tastes a carrot from the garden.

Before watching

Consider these questions:

Who is a child you know well?

What is something that interests you about this child?

Think about different situations where you observed this child. What are some ways that observing in different situations helped you get to know this child better?

While watching

Pay attention to how your knowledge of Jenna increases as you observe her in different situations.

After watching

Take a few minutes to record your thoughts about these questions (you may wish to watch the clip again):

What did you learn about Jenna?

What are some of things you observed Jenna do or say?

What, if anything, did Jenna do or say that interested you?

As a result of what you observed, what questions do you have about her?

As a result of this exercise, what insights do you have?

BRIDGE TO PRACTICE

Remember Randy and the sign he made of Lilian Katz's quote? What might you write on a sign to post in your setting that will help you pay attention to and get to know children better?

Watch, Listen, and Record to See and Remember Details About a Child

When the reason to observe is to build strong, positive relationships with children, details are important. In addition, make sure you watch children in different situations and over an extended period of time. Write notes to help you remember what you see and hear. As you collect these observation notes over the course of days and weeks, you can review them and see how all the information fits together. You are also likely to identify gaps in your knowledge. This will lead you to think of other questions about what else you want to find out to help your relationship unfold and deepen.

 As you watch all the segments of Clip 3, "Jenna, Age 3, in a Variety of Situations" again, use a chart to help you focus on certain details about Jenna. Practice taking some brief observation notes.

Before watching

Recall what you noticed about Jenna when you observed her before. Write a few things you remember seeing Jenna do or say.

While watching

Look carefully for details that convey her individuality. As you observe, use the chart below to record a few words in each category. Use **only** your eyes and ears. Avoid writing your thoughts and feelings. We offer a few examples to get you started. Add more observations to each category.

Actions: **What does Jenna do?**	
Movements: **How does Jenna move?**	*Uses both hands to place and rotate puzzle pieces*
Language: **What does Jenna say?**	
Facial expressions: **How does Jenna move her face?**	*Draws eyebrows together in frown as she works*
Interactions: **What does Jenna do with and say to others?**	*Looks up when Kyla walks by and says, "We're fixing the ball, Kyla."*

After watching

Think about your notes:

How did paying attention to and writing notes about her actions, movements, language, facial expressions, and interactions help you learn about Jenna?

What did you see this time that you missed before?

Reread the words you wrote to see if they are facts that are objective or opinions that are subjective. Answer these questions:

Do your notes describe what **Jenna** actually did or said? Or do they reflect what **you** were thinking or feeling?

If you wrote some words that reflect your own thinking or feelings, think about what you saw that made you write those words. Write what you saw.

Now, return to the notes you wrote about Eliana in Exercise 2. Check them for objectivity. Write some factual words to replace those that describe your own thoughts and feelings.

For the next few days, focus on a child that you do not know particularly well. Use the chart that follows to record details about the child. Observe the child in positive situations, rather than when the child is misbehaving or upset.

Actions: What does the child do?	
Movements: How does the child move?	
Language: What does the child say?	
Facial expressions: How does the child show expression?	
Interactions: What does the child do with and say to others?	

After a few days, consider the following questions:

What do you know about the child now that you did not know before?

How did observing and recording in this way influence your feelings about the child?

How might what you learned affect your relationship with this child?

Reflect to Deepen My Relationship With a Child

Pausing to have a conversation with yourself—to reflect—can help you build and enhance your relationships with children. Take a moment to think about your attitudes and feelings about the child and what the child is doing. Are you feeling positive? Is your reaction negative?

> *Children have an uncanny ability to tune into how you feel about them. They sense your feelings in the way you hold them, the expression on your face, and your tone of voice. Because you play such an important role in their lives, they care about how you feel and they want your approval. Like the ripples caused when you throw a stone into a pond, your feelings about individual children have a far-reaching influence that touches children's developing sense of self, their impressions of and interactions with one another, and even how their parents view you and them.*
>
> (Jablon, Dombro, & Dichtelmiller, 2007)

 We invite you to watch Clip 4, "Alexa, 25 Months, at Work and Play."

Before watching

Think about a child with whom you have a very strong, positive relationship. It can be the same child you thought about earlier in Exercise 5.

What makes your relationship with this child strong? Record three or four factors that have contributed to the strength of your relationship.

Now, think about a child with whom it has been challenging to get to know and build a relationship. Why do you think this has been difficult for you? Record three or four factors that may have made relationship building difficult with this child.

While watching

Write notes about what you see Alexa doing and hear her saying.

After watching

Think about your notes. Use these questions to consider your reactions to and feelings about what you observe. Record your responses:

What did you hear and see that interested you in Alexa and made you want to build a relationship with her? Why?

Was there anything you saw and heard that annoyed you and might get in the way of building a relationship with Alexa? If yes, what was it? Why did it annoy you?

What are two or three concrete steps you might take to get to know her better and build your relationship?

If you are working with others, compare your responses.

Think about characteristics of children that appeal to you and others that annoy you. Discuss this with colleagues and compare your reactions.

How might this exercise help you go beyond your negative reactions to build positive relationships with all children?

Think about a child who has characteristics that make it hard for you to build a relationship. While this is human nature and every one of us has had this experience, building a positive relationship with every child is essential for effective teaching.

As Randy did with Aida, try to find a positive point of connection. Here are some questions to guide you:

What activities does this child choose to do?

What are this child's interests?

What makes this child laugh?

In what situations does this child feel most comfortable?

After observing to answer these questions, try using what you learn to connect with the child and the child's family. Reflect on how your relationship might be shifting. Think about what new insights you have about this child and about yourself.

Respond to Build My Relationship

When your response to children shows respect and appreciation for them, you are fostering positive relationships. To demonstrate respect and appreciation, you might try these strategies:

Use mirror talk. State what you see a child doing, e.g., "You figured out a way to make a tall building that didn't fall down." This is a powerful strategy to connect with a child. Mirror talk gives the child the good feeling of being recognized in a more meaningful way than simply saying, "Good job!" The words you use, the tone of your voice, and the expression on your face together make the child feel validated and appreciated rather than invisible and ignored. Mirror talk shows that you have paid attention to what the child is doing. You can use mirror talk no matter how you feel about a child. It will give you time to notice and put aside any negative feelings so you can be present and responsive.

Use a gesture or facial expression. A thumbs-up, smile, or nod of the head are significant ways to acknowledge what a child is doing and demonstrate your appreciation. These non-verbal affirmations are great to use when you do not want to interrupt what the child is doing but you want the child to know that you are paying attention.

Share with a family member. When you share a child's success or a significant attempt to do something new or difficult, face to face, with a note home, or in a phone call, you let the family and the child know that you really care about what the child does in school. The child gets to see that her family cares too and this doubles her sense of being validated. In this way, the child really experiences you as her advocate.

 View Clip 5, "Aniyah, Age 4, With Her Teacher, Sharon," as Sharon takes dictation, they play a rhyming game, and explore rainbow arches.

Before watching
Think about the opportunities you have every day to nurture your relationships with children. What do you do or say to show respect and appreciation for a child who

does something for the first time?

solves a problem?

shows kindness to another child?

creates a drawing or painting?

does something that makes you smile or laugh?

follows a rule?

While watching

Focus on the relationship between Aniyah and Sharon. Write some notes about all the little and subtle things Sharon says and does to show Aniyah respect and appreciation, which are core aspects of all positive relationships. You might need to watch this clip twice in order to pay close attention to Sharon's actions.

After watching
Review your notes:

In what ways do Sharon's responses to Aniyah contribute to their positive relationship?

How did Sharon use mirror talk and non-verbal acknowledgments with Aniyah?

How might Sharon enhance her relationship with Aniyah's family by communicating information about these exchanges?

How are Sharon's responses similar to or different from what yours might be in similar situations?

What insights do you take away about how your responses to a child can enhance your relationship?

BRIDGE TO PRACTICE

Over the next week, try each of the three ways to respond to build relationships. Record your experiences. What did you try? How did children respond? In what ways is it affecting your relationship?

Use mirror talk to let a child know you are paying attention. Tell the child what you see and hear.

Acknowledge what a child is doing with a gesture or facial expression.

Share what you see with a child's family member so together you can celebrate the child's learning.

What Did I Learn?

What do you want to remember from this chapter about using observation to build relationships with children?

The foundation of a positive relationship is respect and an interest in learning about the uniqueness of the individual. Each child is an incomplete work evolving from a unique set of potentials...It is important to feel and show interest, concern and pleasure in discovering the uniqueness of the individual (Corsini, 1996).

Where Can I Learn More?

Here are some suggestions from *The Power of Observation* (2nd ed.):

"The Power of Positive Relationships," pages 11–13.

"Getting to Know Each Child," pages 13–17.

"Respecting and Appreciating Children," pages 17–19.

"The Powerful Influence of Your Feelings About Children," pages 19–20.

"Connecting With Children," pages 21–22.

"Fostering Children's Success and Competence," pages 23–28.

I Want to Know More About Children's Development and Learning

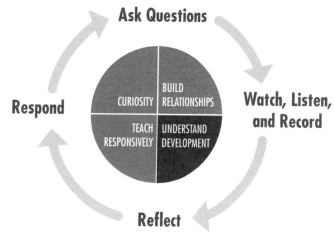

Over the years, we have come to understand that teachers feel pressured to observe children's development and learning because they have been told they must assess what children know and can do. By a certain date, a development and learning checklist must be completed. We are strong believers in the importance of assessment. But too often, assessment functions as an **external** motivation to observe. Paula's desire to observe to teach responsively is an **internal** motivation. Unfortunately, the external pressure to assess children's development and learning often inhibits our internal motivations to observe, that is, our curiosity, our desire to build strong relationships with children, and our efforts to understand their development and learning in order to become more responsive teachers.

Try to resist rushing to focus on development and learning and give yourself the gift of time to wonder and be curious about children and use what you learn to build strong relationships with them. Then you will find that observing to answer questions about development and learning is a natural next step. When you watch and listen to learn everything you can about children's learning styles and their social/emotional, physical, cognitive, and language development, the reward is a deep understanding of and appreciation for individual children. As an added bonus, your assessment results will likely be more informative and accurate!

Thus far, you have read stories about Monique and Randy. Monique's motivation to observe was her curiosity to learn about Jarwin. Randy wanted to have a stronger relationship with Aida, and he observed to find ways to connect with her. Now, you will meet Paula who, in this particular situation is motivated to observe to gain a deep understanding of Jamal's and Alika's development and learning in order to interact with them effectively.

Paula's Story

Paula's story illustrates how she uses the observation cycle to learn more about the development and learning of two children. As we enter Paula's classroom of 4- and 5-year-olds, she is guiding Jamal's and Alika's learning in the block area.

Alika: "Jamal, let's make a big thing."

Jamal: "Okay. I'll get big blocks."

Paula: "What kind of a foundation will this big structure need?"

I have noticed that Alika and Jamal say "thing" to describe many objects. I wonder how they will respond if I introduce new vocabulary?

Alika: "Maybe something big and flat, like the deck we have behind our house."

Jamal: "Yeah, that's a good idea. Let's start with the long ones and put boards on top."

Paula: "Right Jamal, the long quads are great for building the criss-cross way."

Wow. She really understands more vocabulary than she uses. I'll make a note that she understood the word "foundation" and used the word "deck" to explain to Jamal what she wanted to do.

Alika: "Yeah, I did that with Lukas yesterday. It goes like this."

Alika demonstrates with four blocks.

Jamal: "Oh yeah, I can do that. It goes two this way, two that way, two this way."

He gestures with his hands.

Jamal: "Yeah, let's do it that way."

Interesting… Alika demonstrates with blocks and Jamal with words and gestures. I'll add this to my notes.

Paula: "OK, both of you know just what to do!"

They build without talking for several minutes.

Observation: The Key to Responsive Teaching

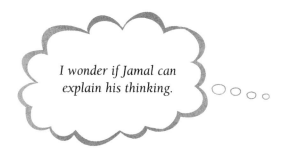

I wonder if Jamal can explain his thinking.

Jamal: "Wow, this is getting big so fast."

Paula: "Yes, it is getting big very fast, Jamal. Why do you think so?"

Jamal: "We put spaces between the long ones. Every row gets higher than the last one."

Alika: "Uh oh, there are only two quads left. What do we do now?"

After a minute, Alika answers her own question.

Alika: "We can just use these shorter ones. Some buildings get skinnier at the top, like the Empire State Building!"

Alika used the word "quad" quickly. I'll make more of an effort to model new words for her and listen to see what happens.

Paula continues to watch, listen, and record a few notes on her clipboard as the children continue to build.

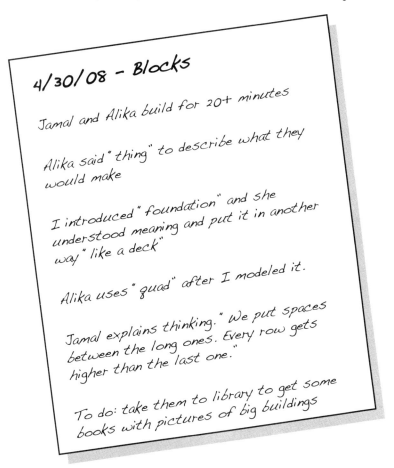

4/30/08 – Blocks

Jamal and Alika build for 20+ minutes

Alika said "thing" to describe what they would make

I introduced "foundation" and she understood meaning and put it in another way "like a deck"

Alika uses "quad" after I modeled it.

Jamal explains thinking. "We put spaces between the long ones. Every row gets higher than the last one."

To do: take them to library to get some books with pictures of big buildings

How does Paula use what she learns from observing to support children's development and learning?

What do you find interesting?

How do you see yourself in the story?

Do you have a similar story to tell?

Practice Observing: I Want to Know More About Children's Development and Learning

Many questions can motivate you to observe to discover how children grow and learn. When you observe in an open way, without a specific agenda, you can learn about many areas of development. For example, when you sit with Sammy at snack time, you might notice details about how he holds his cup (fine motor development), interacts with other children (social development), and how he uses gestures and words to communicate (language development).

At other times, you decide to observe in a more focused way, looking to find answers to questions about one particular area of development. For example, to learn more about Rita's cognitive development, you might choose to observe her as she creates a pattern block design and talk with her about her thinking.

Ask Questions to Find Out About Development and Learning

 Now watch Clip 6, "Observing Development at Different Ages," two times. The first time, for Exercise 9A, you will do an activity to help you develop strategies for open observing. The second time, in Exercise 9B, you will focus on observing social development. The clip includes four short segments, each with two children, ranging in age from 11 months to 5 years.

Exercise 9A: Open Observing

Before watching

Think about each area of development. What is one question in each area of development that motivates you to watch and listen to children?

Social/Emotional Development

Physical Development

Cognitive Development

Language Development

While watching

Make sure that you are observing each area of development so that your questions will be answered. Most people are inclined to focus on certain areas of development more than others because of personal interests, style, or professional knowledge.

As you watch, keep a running tally. Each time you see an area of development in action, make a tally mark in the appropriate row. It might be challenging, but do your best.

Social/Emotional Development _____

Physical Development _____

Cognitive Development _____

Language Development _____

After watching

Discuss your tally marks with others. Think about these questions with one or two colleagues:

What areas did you find you focused on most? Why do you think this is so?

Why might people have different numbers of tally marks for the same area of development?

Look back to the questions you posed about development before watching and share them with your colleagues. Add one or two new questions to your list.

What insights do you have from this exercise?

Exercise 9B: Focused Observing

Before watching

Think about the area of social development. Consider the following questions (*others* refers to both children and adults):

How do children show awareness of and interest in others?

How do children use sounds, language, and/or facial expressions to interact with others?

How do children use physical gestures and actions to interact with others?

How do children show how they feel when they are with other people?

How do children cooperate with others?

What other questions do you have?

While watching

As you watch Clip 6, "Observing Development at Different Ages" again, think about the previous questions related to social development as you take notes about what you see and hear.

After watching

Take a moment to think about what you observed. Put a checkmark beside the questions on the previous page that you answered as you watched the clip. Now, talk with your colleagues. Share both your checkmarks and your observations related to each question.

BRIDGE TO PRACTICE

As you observe children over the next few days, concentrate on the questions you are asking about development and learning.

Do your questions tend to be broad or focused? Do they relate to multiple areas of development or do they focus on one or two areas?

What area(s) of development do you attend to most?

What area(s) of development do you attend to least?

Identify a particular child and observe that child's development and learning for the purpose of learning something new. What did you learn?

Watch, Listen, and Record to Focus on Details About Development and Learning

Many teachers find it helpful to use matrices. A matrix is a grid that allows you to record a word or very brief note to help you recall what you saw and heard. Matrices help you focus on specific skills or behaviors. As they plan a learning experience, they create a matrix with spaces to write the names of the children they plan to observe. They identify four or five learning objectives or behaviors they want to observe during the experience. Doing this helps you focus as you observe.

When your questions focus on children's development and learning, your observations become more specific. You begin to see behaviors such as how a child expresses feelings, grasps a crayon, puts a puzzle together, or phrases questions. Consequently, your notes begin to be more detailed. Over time, it is exciting to notice that your observation notes reveal subtle changes as children grow and learn.

Exercise 10A: Recording With a Matrix

 View Clip 6, "Observing Development at Different Ages."

Before watching
Recall the specific questions about social development you considered. They are now listed as a set of skills in the matrix that follows.

Have you ever used a matrix before?

Did you find it helpful? If so, how?

While watching

Use this matrix to record a few factual words about some aspects of social development. Choose two of the four segments of Clip 6, "Observing Development at Different Ages." We have added a few examples from Segment 6.1, "Alica, 16 Months, and Emma, 11 Months."

Segment 6.1

Write in children's names	Awareness of and interest in others	Use of sounds, language, facial expression to interact with others	Use of physical gestures and actions to interact with others	Evidence of how child feels around others	Demonstrates cooperation
Alicia (pink shirt)			claps hands		
Emma (white shirt)	reaches towards A's tower				

Segment _____

Write in children's names	Awareness of and interest in others	Use of sounds, language, facial expression to interact with others	Use of physical gestures and actions to interact with others	Evidence of how child feels around others	Demonstrates cooperation

Segment _____

Write in children's names	Awareness of and interest in others	Use of sounds, language, facial expression to interact with others	Use of physical gestures and actions to interact with others	Evidence of how child feels around others	Demonstrates cooperation

After watching

Reread your notes and think about these questions:

Do your notes include details?

Are they factual?

Share your matrices with another person. What was similar and different in the ways each of you used each matrix?

Exercise 10B: Using Matrices to See Change Over Time

 View Clip 7, "Melvin, Age 3" in September and October.

Before watching

Think about the social development of a child you have known for several months. Very often change in young children is not obvious. It is gradual and hard to remember, unless you have documented it. Recording observations over time gives you confidence that change has, in fact, taken place. Record a few responses to these questions:

In what ways has the child's social development changed over time? Be specific, e.g., She interacts with more children. She asks to play with a toy instead of grabbing it away from another child. She comes to get my help when she has a problem. She sits in the circle at group time instead of sitting separately.

Have you recorded observations of these changes? If so, how?

While watching

Notice the subtle growth in Melvin's social development from September to October. Use the matrices below to record what you see and hear related to Melvin's social development.

Drawing in September

September	Awareness of and interest in others	Use of sounds, language, facial expression to interact with others	Use of physical gestures and actions to interact with others	Evidence of how child feels around others	Demonstrates cooperation
Melvin					

Making a Collage in October

October	Awareness of and interest in others	Use of sounds, language, facial expression to interact with others	Use of physical gestures and actions to interact with others	Evidence of how child feels around others	Demonstrates cooperation
Melvin					

After watching

Reread your notes and make any changes to them you wish. Consider these questions:

Do you want to add a few more details or make your notes more factual?

Share your matrices with another person. How did the two of you use them in similar and different ways?

What small, subtle changes did you observe in Melvin's social development?

How was using a matrix helpful to you or not helpful?

BRIDGE TO PRACTICE

During the next few weeks, practice using this matrix to observe children's social development. You may want to make another one to help you focus on a different area of development.

Reflect to Understand More About Development and Learning

We have explained that reflection is the conversation you have with yourself that brings meaning to your observations. However, reflecting about development and learning takes time because you are now trying to understand more complex information. Consider these questions.

> *It is not until you observe intently that you find patterns of events and behavior, which might have remained unnoticed.*
>
> (Drummond, 1994)

What area(s) of development or learning did I see? When you reflect you can identify the area of development you have seen. Is it social/emotional development? Physical development? Cognitive development? Language development? Literacy learning? Math learning? Science learning? Social studies learning?

Why is it significant? Was I noticing it for the first time? Does it represent a change from past observations? Is it different from what I usually observe? Am I beginning to see a pattern here?

What are the missing pieces of the puzzle? What else do I need to learn to understand how this child is developing?

At first this may seem impossible to think about while you are observing. For this reason, we encourage you to practice reflecting on development and learning when you have a little time away from your direct work with children. Recognize that it will take time to grow more comfortable thinking about development while observing and interacting with children.

 For this exercise, use Clip 8, "Féfé, Rohil, and Mikey," that includes three short segments. Féfé is 16-months-old and is reading with his caregiver and making music. Rohil, 33-months-old, plays with a Duplo° train. Mikey, 5-years-old, is reading a book to his teacher. As you watch each segment, you will be able to observe multiple areas of development.

Before watching
Quickly review the objectives that guide your curriculum or program. This will help you keep development and learning in mind as you observe. Take a few minutes to think about what you are likely to see children doing in each segment of this clip. Predict what areas of development and learning you are likely to see in action.

Féfé (16 months) reading and making music:

Rohil (33 months) playing with a Duplo train:

Mikey (5 years) reading to his teacher:

While watching

Practice *open* observation. Keep all areas of development in mind as you watch, listen, and record some brief notes. Use this chart to record notes about each child. Remember to be factual and brief while capturing details.

Féfé (16 months)	Sits up on pillow, r leg outstretched holding book moving head/eyes to look at pictures using fingers to turn pages
Rohil (33 months)	
Mikey (5 years)	

After watching

Read your notes and think about these questions:

Do you need to add a few more details or change impressions to facts?

What did you see? Code your notes to help you determine the areas of development you were seeing. Review and mark your notes with the initials of the areas of development.

SE = Social/Emotional development

P = Physical development

C = Cognitive development

L = Language development

Féfé (16 months)	Sits up on pillow, r legs outstretched **P** (gross motor) holding book **P** (fine motor) moving head/eyes to look at pictures **C** (shows interest in the pictures) using fingers to turn pages **P** and **C** (knows that books have pages and you turn the pages to read a book)

What made these observations important enough to record? Share and discuss your notes and codes with another observer. What are the similarities? What are the differences?

What are the missing pieces of the puzzle? Look at your codes. Did you observe all areas of development? Did you observe one or two areas more than others? In which areas of development are your notes most clear and specific? If you could observe the children again, what would you want to learn?

BRIDGE TO PRACTICE

During the next couple of weeks, try coding your notes the way you did in this exercise. The best time to add codes is at the end of each day. It is an excellent way to review and reflect on your observations from the day. In addition, you will find it is easier to code a day's worth of notes rather than a week's worth of notes! Record some notes about your experience.

Respond to Support Children's Development and Learning

Now that you have thought about what you have seen, you can decide how best to respond to support the child's development and learning. Consider two ways to respond.

Interact to scaffold and extend the child's learning. You can help a child move to the next level by responding in these ways:

- Introduce a new tool or material, book, or vocabulary word.

- Join the child's work or play to model a new skill or strategy.

- Offer a suggestion, information, or guidance.

- Use open-ended questions to encourage the child to describe, explain, predict, compare, and contrast.

Make modifications to the program to meet children's needs. To support children's successful exploration, interactions, and learning, you might make changes such as these:

- Adapt the physical environment by moving furniture, changing materials, or altering the ambience (e.g., private places, lowered lighting, cozy corner, softness).

- Adjust the daily schedule and routines.

- Plan learning experiences targeted to individual children's interests and needs.

 For this exercise, use Clip 9, "Responding to Children's Play," which includes two segments. For Exercise 12A, watch Segment 9.1, "Lillian, 23 Months" as she plays with dolls. For Exercise 12B, watch Segment 9.2, "Kyla, Age 5, and Reggie, Age 4." You will see them constructing a ramp for small balls to roll down in the block area.

Exercise 12A: Responding to Lillian

Before watching

Consider how challenging it is to think as you interact with children and make an immediate decision about what to say or do next to support a child's development and maintain his or her interest. You may have developed a routine response that you use in many situations. Maybe you say, "Good job!" and continue walking. You might quiz the child with questions such as, "How many do you have? What color is it? What's that shape?" We react in this way when we feel rushed and do not take the time needed to figure out a more thoughtful and purposeful response.

Think of a situation when you saw a child doing something and you used an automatic response. Share with a colleague. Drawing from the strategies described above, what might you have said or done to respond rather than react?

While watching

Focus on Lillian's development and learning. Record some notes about what you see and hear.

Lillian	*Places dolls face down on floor* *Says, " Nie, nie."*

After watching

Review your notes:

Add a few more details, and check for objectivity.

Using the coding method you learned in Exercise 11, add codes to your observations. This will help you decide how to respond.

How might you respond if this had been a real observation in your classroom? Consider the possible responses below and choose one. Record what you might actually say and/or do in the right-hand column.

How might you respond?	What might you actually say and/or do?	Why would you choose this response?
Interact to scaffold and extend the child's learning. • Introduce a new tool or material, book, or vocabulary word. • Join the child's work or play to model a new skill or strategy. • Offer a suggestion, information or guidance. • Use open-ended questions to encourage the child to describe, explain, predict, compare and contrast.		
Make modifications to the program to meet children's needs. • Adapt the physical environment by moving furniture, changing materials or altering the ambience. • Adjust the daily schedule and routines. • Plan learning experiences targeted to individual children's interests and needs.		

Share your response with another observer:

Discuss your reasons for choosing the response you did. How does your response support development and learning?

Give each other feedback.

How might a child respond to what you decide to do and/or say?

Exercise 12B: Responding to Reggie and Kyla's Play

Repeat Exercise 12A, but this time, use Clip 9, Segment 9.2, "Kyla, Age 5, and Reggie, Age 4."

While watching

Record what you see and hear. You will see two children working together in the block area. You can choose to focus on one child or take some notes about each child.

Kyla	
Reggie	

After watching

Review your notes:

Add a few more details, and check for objectivity.

Using the coding method you learned in Exercise 11, add codes to your observations. This will help you decide how to respond.

How might you respond if this had been a real observation in your classroom? Consider the possible responses below and choose one. Record what you might actually say and/or do in the columns to the right.

How might you respond?	What might you actually say and/or do?	Why would you choose this response?
Interact to scaffold and extend the child's learning. • Introduce a new tool or material, book, or vocabulary word. • Join the child's work or play to model a new skill or strategy. • Offer a suggestion, information or guidance. • Use open-ended questions to encourage the child to describe, explain, predict, compare and contrast.		
Make modifications to the program to meet children's needs. • Adapt the physical environment by moving furniture, changing materials or altering the ambience. • Adjust the daily schedule and routines. • Plan learning experiences targeted to individual children's interests and needs.		

During the next few days, think about development and learning as you observe. Try to use the two types of responses that you practiced in this exercise.

What Did I Learn?

What do you want to remember from this chapter about using observation to learn more about children's development and learning?

Where Can I Learn More?

Here are some suggestions from *The Power of Observation* (2nd ed.):

"Observe Over Time," pages 56–58.

"Watch Children in Varied Situations," pages 58–60.

Using matrices, rating scales, tallies, diagrams, sketches and photographs, audiotapes and videotapes to record what you see, pages 80–84.

"Making Your Program Responsive to Children," pages 97–102.

I Want to Teach More Responsively

As you have seen, curiosity is a powerful reason to observe children, no matter how well you know them. When you observe to help you build relationships with individual children, you make connections. These connections guide your efforts to give children a safe and trusting foundation from which they can explore. By paying attention to children's development and learning, you enrich your understanding of them. This greater understanding allows you to consider how best to respond to them. This leads to the fourth reason to observe: becoming a more responsive teacher.

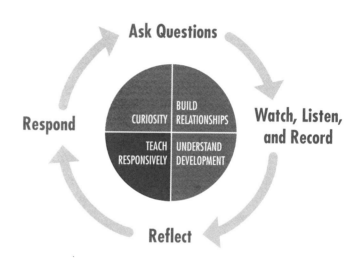

You might be asking, how is being a more responsive teacher different from the fourth phase of the observation cycle, respond? We respond to children all the time. However, teaching responsively means thinking about the subtle variations in how children interact with you. You can begin to customize your language, actions, and gestures to correspond to the preferences of each child. The knowledge you gain from observing makes you a more responsive teacher by helping you decide about when, what, and how to teach. This knowledge improves the quality of guidance and instruction you are able to offer individual children. After careful and purposeful observing, you can pay attention to how individual children respond to your guidance, intervention, and assistance. You can see that verbal cues are effective for some children and non-verbal cues are more effective for others. This is the essence of good teaching.

The wealth of information you have on each child is only meaningful if it is linked to decisions about teaching. It can help you plan for children individually and for your group as a whole.

(Dodge, Colker, & Heroman, 2002)

Sandra's Story

Here's a story about Sandra. Notice how she uses what she has learned from observing to inform how she interacts with and teaches 2-year-old Zachary.

It is lunchtime in the toddler room. Zachary has a plate of food in front of him: pieces of cheese, wedges of apple, a few cherry tomatoes, cucumber slices, and some crackers. He stares at the plate without reaching for any food.

Sandra: "Zach, you're looking at your plate of food. You have a lot of things to choose from. Would you like to start with some cheese or apple?"

I'll use mirror talk, so Zach knows I'm paying attention to him. I've noticed that he responds well when I offer choices.

Zachary points to the cheese and looks at Sandra.

Sandra: "Cheese. I've seen you eat cheese a lot. You must like it!"

Zachary picks up a piece of cheese, says "eeze," and puts it in his mouth. He eats two pieces of cheese, then eats an apple wedge, and stops eating.

Sandra: "You're looking at your plate again. You still have a lot of choices. Show me which food you're going to choose next."

Zachary points to the crackers, saying "aks."

Sandra: "I didn't know you knew how to say crackers. I'm going to write a note about that and tell your dad about your new word!"

I want to encourage Zach's language development by calling attention to his new words and let him know that this is exciting enough to tell his father.

Zach's language development seems to be in a real growth period right now. I need to expose him to some new words each day.

Zachary munches on various things on his plate for several minutes and then points to the cup in front of Maria who is sitting next to him. "Ick, ick," he says.

Sandra: "Oh Zachary, you're telling me you'd like some milk and we forgot to give you some. Just last week, you would have cried for more milk and now you are asking with words. You are growing so fast, it's hard to keep track. Watch this. I'm writing "Zachary asked for milk at lunch today!" I can't wait to hear the new words you say next week!"

Zachary watches Sandra and grins.

WHAT DO YOU THINK?

How did Sandra observe and teach responsively?

What do you find interesting?

How do you see yourself in the story?

Do you have a similar story to tell?

Practice Observing: I Want to Teach More Responsively

Until now, your questions have been about children. When your motivation for observing is responsive teaching, there are new questions to ask. How do individual children respond to my guidance and instruction? How can I use this information to make sure that my responses are effective for each child?

Examples of specific questions you might ask include these:

- What do I do to elicit positive behaviors from each child?

- What do I do that causes negative behaviors from each child?

- How might I change the environment to enhance positive behaviors and lessen negative behaviors?

- How does each child respond to different ways I use my voice?

- How should I present information so that the listeners, lookers, and movers all benefit?

- What special attention might a child need to experience success in a particular situation?

Ask Questions to Teach Responsively

 For this exercise, watch Clip 10, "Daily Routines." You will see toileting in a toddler room, lunchtime in a Head Start Program with 4-year-olds, and choosing books before morning meeting with 4-year-olds in a public preschool program.

Before watching

Think about routines. Routines include arrival, group time, choice time, clean-up time, snack and meal times, rest/nap time, outdoor time, end-of-the-day, and departure. The energy level, mood, sociability, flexibility, perseverance, patience, and curiosity of any given child may change throughout the day and from day to day. And it is likely that no two children will respond in the same way to any given part of a day. To ensure that every child has positive learning experiences during all parts of each day, rely on what you can learn from observing to help you.

Choose one routine to think about. Think of two children who respond in different ways to this routine. Record your thoughts on the following chart.

Daily routine: _____

Children's initials	Describe how each child typically responds to this routine. Use facts, not judgments. Consider energy level, mood, sociability, flexibility, perseverance, patience, and curiosity, etc.	Look back at the previous questions. Which might you ask to support this child during this routine? Or, is there another question you might ask?
Child #1:		
Child #2:		

Discuss your responses with a colleague and record some notes.

While watching

In each segment of Clip 10, "Daily Routines," look carefully at what happens between teachers and individual children. Look for examples that show how teachers adjust what they say or do based on what they observe.

Teacher	Examples of Individualizing Interactions Based on Observations
Taisha **How does she guide Cooper to both cooperate and feel independent?**	*Says, "Here Cooper, pull up your pants."*
Nory **How does she adjust what she says and does to make lunch time comfortable for each child?**	
Adam **How does he individualize his responses as children choose books before morning meeting?**	

After watching

Share your observations and notes with another observer. Look for similarities and differences. Think about and discuss how you might apply what you saw to your practice.

Observation: The Key to Responsive Teaching

Post the list of questions from this exercise (see below) in a place where you will read them every day. Refer to them as you observe children during routines. Look for ways your responses are becoming more individualized.

Questions to Help Me Be a Responsive Teacher

What can I do to elicit positive behaviors from each child?

What do I do that causes negative behaviors from each child?

How might I change the environment to enhance positive behaviors and lessen negative behaviors?

How does each child respond to different ways I use my voice?

How should I present information so that the listeners, lookers, and movers all benefit?

What special attention might a child need to experience success in a particular situation?

Watch, Listen, and Record to Teach Responsively

When observing for the purpose of teaching responsively, the notes you record need to include references to what you, the teacher or provider, do or say in addition to noting what the child does and says. This helps you remember the interactions you have and the effect they have on children.

In Clip 11, "Teacher-Child Interactions," you will view two segments. For Exercise 14A, watch Segment 11.1, "Tara, 24 Months and Her Teacher, Elaine." They are playing a game of hello and goodbye. For Exercise 14B, watch Segment 11.2, "Klaudia, Age 5, and Her Teacher, Louis." Klaudia is investigating bubbles on the playground.

Exercise 14A: Observing an Interaction Between a Teacher and a Toddler

Before watching

Read the following two examples of observation notes that document an interaction between a teacher and 3-year-old Carley, who is building with Legos®. In the example on the right, *C* stands for Carley and *M* stands for Maria, the teacher.

Carley – 5-26-08	*5-26-08*
begins collecting 3-inch blue Legos, puts them in pile	*C: collects 3-inch blue Legos, puts in pile*
I help	*M: Would you like help?*
says " In the middle"	*C: nods - says Yes.*
clears area in center of table	*M: We made need a big space. Where shall we put them all?*
says " a boat"	*C: says, " In the middle" & clears area in center of table*
says " Derek"	
heads toward D	*We make a big pile legos in silence for few minutes.*
takes him by the hand	*M: What are you thinking about building with all these blue Legos?*
brings him to table	
says " play with me? make a boat?"	*C: a boat*
Derek nods yes	*M: Do you want someone to help you?*
they begin working	*C: yes*
	M: Who would you like to ask? Who's good at building with Legos?
	C: " Derek" heads toward D, takes him by the hand, brings him to table, " play with me? make a boat?"
	Derek nods yes & the work begins

Consider and discuss these questions with others:

In what ways are the two records the same?

How are they different?

In what ways might each record help the teacher intentionally plan for positive interactions with Carley in the future?

What insights do you take from this comparison of note-taking?

While watching

As you watch Segment 11.1, practice recording a teacher-child interaction. Use *T* to stand for Tara, the child and *E* for Elaine, the teacher. Record the interaction here:

After watching

Review your notes, add a few more details, and check for objectivity. Consider these ideas:

Share your notes with another observer. Compare and contrast. Look for similarities and differences.

Discuss this question: What are some advantages to recording both sides of teacher-child interactions?

Exercise 14B: Observing an Interaction Between a Teacher and a Five-Year-Old Child

In this part of the exercise you have a chance to practice observing and documenting another teacher-child interaction, this time between Louis, the teacher, and Klaudia, age 5. Use Segment 11.2.

Before watching

Take a moment to review your notes about the interaction between Elaine and Tara in Exercise 14A:

Is there some way you might improve upon them?

Do you want to add more details or more about what the teacher said?

Observation: The Key to Responsive Teaching

While watching

Record your notes as you did in Exercise 14A. Use *L* for Louis and *K* for Klaudia.

After watching

Review your notes, add a few more details, and check for objectivity. Then, share and respond to these suggestions and questions:

Share your notes with another observer. Compare and contrast. Look for similarities and differences.

How did this observation experience differ from the first one?

What were some examples of ways Louis had a positive influence on Klaudia's behavior and/or learning?

During the next week or so, record some notes during interactions with children. Try to capture the essence of your words and actions as well as the responses of the child. In order to do this, you are likely to discover that you will need to slow the pace of your interactions. Do not worry about this. Taking the time to record notes also gives you time to think about the next part of your interaction. Refer to "Questions to Help Me Be a Responsive Teacher" from Exercise 13 on page 73 as you make decisions about how to individualize your interactions with children.

Observing slows me down. I listen to children more. I engage with them instead of teaching at them.

(Jablon, Dombro, & Dichtelmiller, 2007)

Reflect to Teach Responsively

In the midst of observing and interacting, we have asked you to pause and think, have a mental conversation with yourself, be aware of your attitudes and feelings towards children, and focus on development and learning, so that you can respond with intention.

At this moment, you might be saying to yourself, *Let me get this straight. You think I can interact with children, observe, take notes, AND do all these other things? I'm not some kind of super-human being!* Yes, we know it IS a lot to ask, but it is doable with patience, practice with colleagues, and an open mind. Remember, good teachers are curious, life-long learners.

 For this exercise, use Clip 12, "Taking Time to Think." Although five short segments are included in this clip, begin with Segment 12.1, "Henry, 4 Months, and His Teacher, Marjorie" for Exercise 15A. Then, choose two or three additional segments to practice in Exercise 15B. Be sure to pause between each segment.

Exercise 15A: Watching Marjorie Use Mirror Talk With Henry

Before watching
Take a deep breath, always a good strategy to remember to use before you begin observing. Do you remember reading about mirror talk in Chapter 3? Look back to page 36 to refresh your memory.

While watching
Notice how Marjorie uses mirror talk with Henry. Think about how she uses this strategy for many purposes.

After watching
Consider the following questions:

How does Marjorie use mirror talk to express her curiosity and share it with Henry's mom?

How does Marjorie use mirror talk to build a relationship with Henry and his mother?

How does Marjorie use mirror talk to focus attention on Henry's development and learning?

Exercise 15B: Reflecting On What I See

Choose to watch two or three additional short segments from Clip 12, "Taking Time to Think."

Before watching
Remember that we have encouraged you to give yourself time to think as you watch and interact with children at work and play. In this next exercise, give yourself permission to focus on what **you** are thinking as you watch the child. Rather than noting what you see and hear the child do, concentrate on your mental conversation.

While watching
In each segment, you will see a child or children playing independently. As you watch, imagine you are there and allow yourself time to think about what you see:

Note what you are curious about.

Think about building a relationship with this child. What are your attitudes and feelings about the child?

Identify aspects of development and learning that you see.

Observation: The Key to Responsive Teaching

After watching

Share your thoughts with a colleague:

What did you think about?

How was it the same or different from your colleagues?

Why do you think so?

BRIDGE TO PRACTICE

When you are with children, practice reflection in this way. Take a deep breath and ask yourself these questions. Record your thoughts:

Was it about your curiosity?

Was it about building a relationship with this child? Were you thinking about your attitudes and feelings about the child?

Were you thinking about aspects of development and learning that you saw?

Respond to Teach Effectively

You have made it to the final exercise. Throughout this book we have discussed many different ways to respond. Some you already do and others may be new to you. Reflecting about what you observe leads to responses that are more intentional and purposeful. You may respond immediately or make a plan to carry out in the future. Deciding how to respond is like being at a crossroad where you stop and consider which way to go. There are basically three directions you can go with your response. They connect to the reasons for observing. Whichever direction you choose, you have some options about how to proceed.

You are curious and want to learn more about the child. You may consider these responses:

- Continue to observe and document what you see and hear.

- Make a plan to observe in a different situation.

- Ask a family member a question to get more information.

You want to build a relationship with the child. You may consider these responses:

- Use mirror talk to let the child know you are paying attention. Tell the child what you see and hear.

- Acknowledge what a child is doing with a gesture or facial expression. A thumbs up or a smile can help to validate a child's experience.

- Share what you see with a member of a child's family so together you can celebrate the child's learning.

You want to promote the child's development and learning. You may respond in these ways:

- Interact to scaffold and extend the child's learning—

  Introduce a new tool or material, book, or vocabulary word.

  Join the child's work or play to model a new skill or strategy.

  Offer a suggestion, information or guidance.

  Use open-ended questions to encourage the child to describe, explain, predict, compare, and contrast.

- Make modifications to the program to meet children's needs—

  Adapt the physical environment by moving furniture, changing materials or altering the ambience.

  Adjust the daily schedule and routines.

  Plan learning experiences targeted to individual children's interests and needs.

Now you have an opportunity to practice! For this exercise, watch Clip 13, "Jonathan, Age 3, and His Teacher, Jamie."

Before watching

Reflect on ways you are responsive to individual children as you teach. Look at the list of responses on the previous page in relation to your practice.

While watching

Think about how Jamie teaches Jonathan responsively. Notice and make notes about how she uses these strategies:

- She is curious and open to learning more about Jonathan.

- She shows respect and appreciation to build a relationship with Jonathan.

- She promotes Jonathan's development and learning.

After watching

Share your reactions to Jamie and Jonathan with a colleague. Compare your notes. If you were Jonathan's teacher, what might you have done differently?

Congratulations! You have completed sixteen exercises and are ready for chapter 6. This chapter will help you make the transition from this Workbook to your own practice.

What Did I Learn?

What important ideas from this chapter about observing to teach responsively do you want to remember?

An important part of my job is to be a keen observer of children. As I interact with children, I watch to see what they know and can do, and then tell them what I see. Then I create a challenge that pushes them, but yet is still attainable. I want them to have the opportunity to feel and be successful. Carol, Preschool Teacher

Where Can I Learn More?

Here are some suggestions from *The Power of Observation* (2nd ed.):

"Responding to Individuals and the Group," pages 103–104.

"Supporting Individual Children," pages 105–109.

"Responding to the Group," pages 109–111.

"Balancing Individual and Group Needs," pages 112–116.

"Responding to Challenging Behaviors," pages 116–122.

"Working Together With Families," pages 132–140.

Observing to Be a Responsive Teacher: What's Next For You?

Together we have been on a journey exploring how the power of observation can help you become a more responsive teacher. By reading and doing exercises, sharing questions and discoveries with colleagues, and using bridges to practice, you have had opportunities to validate and build on what you know about observing. We hope you have also refined your skills and developed new ones.

This is a good time to consider where you are on your way toward becoming an effective observer and a responsive teacher. Begin by assessing your knowledge, attitudes, and skills using the tool below. Then decide on the next steps for you. Try to be honest with yourself. Remember, becoming a good observer and a responsive teacher is an ongoing process. No matter how much experience you have, there is always something new to learn.

Where Are You on Your Journey?

Observation deserves as much time and attention as anything else in your day. It can help you satisfy your curiosity, build relationships with children, learn about children's development, and become a more responsive teacher.

We have organized questions around the four reasons to observe. Remember, the first three reasons: curiosity, relationship building, and development and learning, all build on each other as they guide you to the fourth reason, responsive teaching. Think about and respond to the questions that follow.

Observing Because You Are Curious

1. How difficult or easy is it for you to **ask questions** and be curious about each child in your group?

1	2	3	4
quite difficult	slightly difficult	easy	very easy

2. How frequently are you **watching, listening, and recording** notes to find answers to your questions about each child?

1	2	3	4
never	rarely	sometimes	frequently

3. Reflection requires you to slow down and listen to your internal conversation. To what extent has **reflection** helped you be more able to see children in new ways?

1	2	3	4
not at all	a little	somewhat	significantly

4. To pursue your curiosity about children, you can **respond** to your observations in three ways. How often do you use each of these three responses to satisfy your curiosity about children?

4a. I continue to observe and document a child's learning.

1	2	3	4
never	rarely	sometimes	frequently

4b. I observe a child in different situations.

1	2	3	4
never	rarely	sometimes	frequently

4c. I ask questions and learn from family members.

1	2	3	4
never	rarely	sometimes	frequently

Observing to Build Relationships

5. How difficult or easy is it for you to **ask questions** to get to know each child better and look for positive points of connection?

1	2	3	4
quite difficult	slightly difficult	easy	very easy

6. How frequently do you **watch, listen, and record** factual details in order to get know each child extremely well?

1	2	3	4
never	rarely	sometimes	frequently

7. To what extent has **reflection** helped you to recognize when you have negative feelings about a child and allowed you to go beyond these feelings so you can build a positive relationship?

1	2	3	4
not at all	a little	somewhat	considerably

8. To build positive relationships with children, how often do you **respond** in the following ways?

8a. I use mirror talk.

1	2	3	4
never	rarely	sometimes	frequently

8b. I acknowledge what a child says or does with a gesture or facial expression.

1	2	3	4
never	rarely	sometimes	frequently

8c. I share an observation with a child's family member.

1	2	3	4
never	rarely	sometimes	frequently

Observing to Understand Development and Learning

9. How difficult or easy is it for you to **ask questions** that guide your observations about each child's development and learning?

1	2	3	4
quite difficult	slightly difficult	easy	very easy

10. How difficult or easy is it for you to **watch, listen, and record** to gather information about each child's development and learning?

1	2	3	4
quite difficult	slightly difficult	easy	very easy

11. To **reflect** on each child's development and learning, how frequently do you ask yourself these questions:

11a. What areas of development am I seeing?

1	2	3	4
never	rarely	sometimes	frequently

11b. Why is this observation significant?

1	2	3	4
never	rarely	sometimes	frequently

11c. What are the missing pieces of the puzzle?

1	2	3	4
never	rarely	sometimes	frequently

12. How often do you **respond** in the following ways to promote each child's development and learning?

12a. I interact to scaffold and extend the child's learning.

1	2	3	4
never	rarely	sometimes	frequently

12b. I make appropriate modifications to the program.

1	2	3	4
never	rarely	sometimes	frequently

Observing to Teach Responsively

13. When your motivation for observing is responsive teaching, you **ask questions** about how each child is responding to your guidance and instruction. How difficult or easy is it for you to ask such questions to guide your observations?

1	2	3	4
quite difficult	slightly difficult	easy	very easy

14. How difficult or easy is it for you to **watch, listen, and record** to gather information about how each child is responding to your guidance and instruction?

1	2	3	4
quite difficult	slightly difficult	easy	very easy

15. How frequently do you give yourself time to **reflect** so that you can understand what children are doing and learning and make informed decisions about how best to respond?

1	2	3	4
never	rarely	sometimes	frequently

16. Teaching responsively means basing your decisions on observation and reflection, rather than simply reacting. How often do you use what you learn from observing children to individualize how you **respond**?

1	2	3	4
never	rarely	sometimes	frequently

General Observation Questions

17. How frequently do you observe and record?

1	2	3	4
never	rarely	sometimes	frequently

18. To what extent does your note-taking system give you the information you need to be a responsive teacher?

1	2	3	4
not at all	a little	somewhat	considerably

19. How frequently do you share and discuss observations with team members?

1	2	3	4
never	rarely	sometimes	frequently

20. How frequently do you share and discuss observations with family members?

1	2	3	4
never	rarely	sometimes	frequently

Where Are You Going Next?

To recognize your professional growth, revisit the self-assessment questions periodically to observe your progress. As you reflect on your journey to use observation for responsive teaching, we encourage you to think about the four phases of the observation cycle. What action(s) do you want to take for each phase:

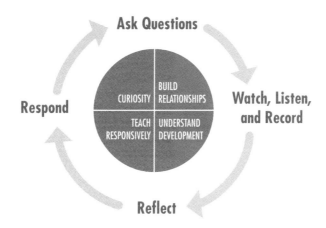

1. **Asking questions**: (Self-Assessment Questions 1, 5, 9, 13)
   My next steps are:

2. **Watching, listening and recording**: (Self-Assessment Questions 2, 6, 10, 14, 17, 18)
   My next steps are:

3. **Reflecting**: (Self-Assessment Questions 3, 7, 11, 15, 19)
   My next steps are:

4. **Responding:** (Self-Assessment Questions 4, 8, 12, 16, 20)
   My next steps are:

Closing Thoughts

Your days are busy and we know that. You might wonder then, why we end this book with a list of next steps for you take. It is because observing is at the core of responsive teaching. It is a mindset and skill that deserves as much time and attention as anything else you do in the course of a day. Only by observing can you gain the knowledge you need to make decisions that can make a positive difference in the lives of children and families. They will benefit and so will you as your work becomes even more interesting and rewarding.

Appendix A
Exercises and Clips

Exercise 1: Clip 1, A Collage of Young Children

Segment 1.1: Henry, 4 Months

Segment 1.2: Alicia, 16 Months

Segment 1.3: Tara, 24 Months

Segment 1.4: Jonathan, Age 3

Segment 1.5: Mikey, Age 5, and Boris, Age 4

Segment 1.6: Klaudia and Kimberly, Age 5

Exercises 2, 3, and 4: Clip 2, Eliana, Age 4

Segment 2.1: Eliana Draws During Choice Time (Exercises 2 and 3)

Segment 2.2: Eliana With Puppets (Exercise 4)

Exercises 5 and 6: Clip 3, Jenna, Age 3, in a Variety of Situations

Segment 3.1: Jenna Arrives at Preschool

Segment 3.2: Jenna Works on a Puzzle

Segment 3.3: Jenna Pumps a Ball

Segment 3.4: Jenna Washes a Rubber Animal and Sings a Song

Segment 3.5: Jenna Washes and Tastes a Carrot

Exercise 7: Clip 4, Alexa, 25 Months, at Work and Play

Exercise 8: Clip 5, Aniyah, Age 4, With Her Teacher, Sharon

Segment 5.1: Sharon Takes Dictation for Aniyah

Segment 5.2: Aniyah Plays a Rhyming Game With Sharon

Segment 5.3: Aniyah and Sharon With Rainbow Arches

Exercises 9A, 9B, and 10A: Clip 6, Observing Development at Different Ages

Segment 6.1: Alicia, 16 Months, and Emma, 11 Months

Segment 6.2: Cooper and Olivia, 21 Months

Segment 6.3: Grace, Age 5, and Alexis, Age 3

Segment 6.4: Jesery and Aniyah, Age 4

Exercise 10B: Clip 7, Melvin, Age 3

Segment 7.1: Melvin in September

Segment 7.2: Melvin in October

Exercise 11: Clip 8, Féfé, Rohil, and Mikey

Segment 8.1: Féfé, 16 Months

Segment 8.2: Rohil, 33 Months

Segment 8.3: Mikey, Age 5

Exercise 12: Clip 9, Responding to Children's Play

Segment 9.1: Lillian, 23 Months (Exercise 12A)

Segment 9.2: Kyla, Age 5, and Reggie, Age 4 (Exercise12B)

Exercise 13: Clip 10, Daily Routines

Segment 10.1: Toddlers' Toileting

Segment 10.2: Four-Year-Old Children Having Lunch

Segment 10.3: Choosing Books Before Morning Meeting

Exercise 14: Clip 11, Teacher-Child Interactions

Segment 11.1: Tara, 24 Months, and Her Teacher, Elaine (Exercise 14A)

Segment 11.2: Klaudia, Age 5, and Her Teacher, Louis (Exercise 14B)

Exercise 15: Clip 12, Taking Time to Think

Segment 12.1: Henry, 4 Months, and His Teacher, Marjorie (Exercise15A)

Segment 12.2: Olivia, 21 Months (Exercise 15B)

Segment 12.3: Adam, Age 4 (Exercise 15B)

Segment 12.4: Max and Emily, Age 4 (Exercise 15B)

Segment 12.5: Adelina, Age 4 (Exercise 15B)

Exercise 16: Clip 13, Jonathan, Age 3, and His Teacher, Jamie

Appendix B
Resources and References

Although not comprehensive, this list includes resources that have been especially helpful to us in our work as teachers and staff developers.

On Observing

Bentzen, W. R. (2004). *Seeing young children: A guide to observing and recording behavior* (5th ed.). Clifton Park, NY: Delmar.

> This guide provides detailed information about observing and recording young children's behavior. Many different recording techniques and instruments are included.

Colker, L. J. (1995). *Observing young children: Learning to look, looking to learn.* Washington, DC: Teaching Strategies, Inc.

> This video focuses on teaching objective observation skills and how to apply them in the classroom setting. It describes a number of techniques and walks you through several practice observations.

On Teachers as Curious Learners

Perry, R. (1998). *Teaching practice.* London: Routledge.

> This book challenges teachers to do their own thinking about learning and teaching, encouraging them to apply their specialized and personal knowledge to the development of sound teaching practices and dynamic learning environments.

Fried, R. (2001). *The passionate teacher: A practical guide* (2nd ed.). Boston: Beacon Press.

> This book offers stories and ideas about how to be a curious, passionate learner while being an effective teacher. Fried provides many strategies about how to discover children's interests and use them as the basis for teaching.

On Building Positive, Trusting Relationships With Children

Howes, C., & Ritchie, S. (2002). *A matter of trust: Connecting teachers and learners in early childhood classrooms.* New York: Teachers College Press.

> Howes and Ritchie detail the nature of interactions between children and their teachers that promote trust and account for positive learning outcomes.

Jablon, J. R., Dombro, A. L., & Dichtelmiller, M. L. (2007). *The power of observation* (2nd ed.). Washington, DC: Teaching Strategies, Inc. and National Association for the Education of Young Children.

> The link between observation and building relationships is an important theme of this book. The authors share their own experiences and those of many others to illustrate how observation helps teachers and caregivers become more effective in the child care center, preschool, family child care home, or elementary classroom. It offers guidelines for effective observation and specific strategies to help you refine your observation skills and transform observing into an integral part of your teaching.

On Understanding and Promoting Children's Development and Learning

Shonkoff, J. P., & Philips, D. A. (Eds.) (2000). *From neurons to neighborhoods: The science of early childhood development.* Washington, DC: National Academy Press.

> While reflecting the thinking and work of respected scientists, *From Neurons to Neighborhoods* is an accessible read. It presents the evidence about "brain wiring" and how children learn to speak, think, and regulate their behavior. It examines the effect of the climate—family, child care, community—within which the child grows.

Gronlund, G., & James, M. (2005). *Focused observations: How to observe children for assessment and curriculum planning.* St. Paul, MN: Redleaf Press.

> *Focused Observations* suggests practical ways for teachers to use observation purposefully and regularly. It not only provides teachers with strategies to help them make observation an integral part of their teaching, but it also focuses on how observations can inform assessment, program planning, and the conduct of case studies. A trainer's DVD is also available.

www.zerotothree.org This Web site offers a comprehensive interactive resource for early childhood education professionals and families. The Web site's primary purpose is to enhance the understanding and promotion of healthy development of children ages zero to three.

On Responsive Teaching

Curtis, D., & Carter, M. (2000). *The art of awareness: How observation can transform your teaching.* St. Paul, MN: Redleaf Press.

> *The Art of Awareness* helps teachers learn to use observation to enhance their appreciation of children's individuality and use what they learn to respond to each child effectively. The book is both practical and inspirational.

Epstein, A. S. (2007). *The intentional teacher: Choosing the best strategies for young children's learning.* Washington, DC: National Association for the Education of Young Children.

> Epstein describes how teachers use knowledge and purpose to make sure young children acquire the skills and understanding they need to succeed. *The Intentional Teacher* explores how and when to use three types of learning (child-guided, adult-guided, or a combination).

References

Chapter 2:

Leipzig, J. (Summer 1988).
   Being there. *Day care and early education*, 15(4), 37.

Chapter 3:

Corsini, D. (1996).
   Developing positive relationships with children. In Eller, C. L. (Ed.), *School-Age Connections*, 5(3),
   Storrs, CT: University of Connecticut Cooperative Extension System.
   http://www.nncc.org/Prof.Dev/sac53_develop.pos.relat.html

Jablon, J. R., Dombro, A.L., & Dichtelmiller, M. L. (2007).
   The power of observation (2nd ed.). Washington, DC: Teaching Strategies, Inc. and
   National Association for the Education of Young Children, pp. 11, 19.

Katz, L., personal communication, June 10, 2008.

Chapter 4:

Drummond, M. J. (1994).
   Learning to see: Assessment through observation, York, Maine: Stenhouse Publishers, p. 57.

Chapter 5:

Dodge, D. T., Colker, L. J., & Heroman, C. (2002).
   The Creative Curriculum for preschool (4th ed.). Washington, DC: Teaching Strategies, Inc., p. 206.

Jablon, J. R., Dombro, A.L., & Dichtelmiller, M. L. (2007). *The power of observation* (2nd ed.). Washington,
   DC: Teaching Strategies, Inc. and National Association for the Education of Young Children, p.12.

Teaching Strategies, Inc. strives to improve the quality of early childhood programs by producing comprehensive and practical curriculum and training materials. Our products and staff development services are making a difference in preschools, elementary schools, Head Start, school-age programs, and child care programs worldwide.

The Power of Observation, 2nd ed.
Explores the vital connection between observing and effective teaching. The new edition features expanded guidance on applying your observations to your daily practices and includes a study guide.
#CB1522, $24.95

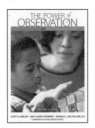

The Creative Curriculum® for Preschool
This fully updated edition keeps its original environmentally-based approach and clearly defines the teacher's vital role in connecting content, teaching, and learning.
#CB0019, $49.95
Also available in Spanish: #CB0155, $49.95

The Creative Curriculum® for Infants, Toddlers & Twos, 2nd ed.
This comprehensive curriculum helps teachers create the very best program for children under age 3. The new edition retains its focus on building relationships, responsive care, and routines and experiences while updating the curriculum in many new ways.
#CB7996, $49.95
Also available in Spanish: #CB1409, $49.95

Building the Primary Classroom: A Complete Guide to Teaching and Learning
Provides the organizational and practical strategies primary teachers need to build great classrooms. Includes six strategies for teaching and learning: Knowing the Children You Teach, Building a Classroom Community, Establishing a Structure for the Classroom, Guiding Children's Learning, Assessing Children's Learning, and Building a Partnership with Families.
#CB0088, $49.95

The Creative Curriculum® for Preschool Developmental Continuum Assessment Toolkit
An integrated assessment system using a valid and reliable instrument—*The Creative Curriculum® Developmental Continuum for Ages 3–5.* Provides tools to collect data and analyze children's progress as part of demonstrating program outcomes. Boxed set contains forms to record progress for a class at three checkpoints each year.
#CB0130, $114.95
Also available in Spanish: #CB0142, $114.95

The Creative Curriculum® for Preschool in Action! DVD
This DVD provides an in-depth examination of *The Creative Curriculum® for Preschool* and shows how teachers use it to guide their thinking and decision making about teaching and learning. Filmed in a variety of Head Start and child care settings, each section is ideal for ongoing teacher study groups and parent workshops. Includes English and Spanish captioning and a bonus: the classic 1988 version of *The Creative Curriculum® Video.*
#CB1508, $199.95

Literacy: The Creative Curriculum® Approach
Preschool literacy experiences should be intentionally built into the entire daily schedule and all interest areas in the classroom. This book shows you how to maximize literacy learning opportunities within the context of a comprehensive, integrated curriculum. This book supplements *The Creative Curriculum® for Preschool.*
#CB7877, $44.95

Mathematics: The Creative Curriculum® Approach
Young children love mathematics and are interested in numbers, shapes, sizes, and patterns. The preschool teacher can use these interests to purposefully build mathematical knowledge and understanding by carefully planning lessons and maximizing learning in interest areas and throughout the day. Children will thus learn math as part of a comprehensive, integrated curriculum. This book supplements *The Creative Curriculum® for Preschool.*
#CB7880, $44.95

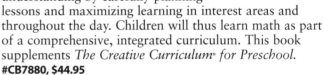

CreativeCurriculum.net
A complete online version of our assessment and outcomes reporting tools. Includes individual child profiles, group planning reports, parent communication features, and activities for each child. For a free 30-day trial, visit www.CreativeCurriculum.net.

The Creative Curriculum® for Infants, Toddlers & Twos Developmental Continuum Assessment Toolkit
This ongoing, authentic assessment system is based on *The Creative Curriculum® Developmental Continuum for Infants, Toddlers & Twos.* Its 21 objectives provide the tools to collect and analyze data and track young children's progress.
#CB7897, $139.95
Also available in Spanish: CB1492, $139.95

Order online at our Web site, www.TeachingStrategies.com, or call 800-637-3652 or 301-634-0818.